PIECES OF ME

KINJAL UTTEKAR

notionpress.com

INDIA · SINGAPORE · MALAYSIA

ISBN 979-8-89002-987-4

For,
those whose stories have
inspired and shaped this book.
Your love and support have been invaluable
and are my greatest prize.

*These pieces of me are
the chaos within my core....*

Contents

MY HEART

Masterpiece 11

Soulmate 13

Hopeful 14

With You 15

Mother 17

Friendship 20

Love 22

You and me 24

Sail 25

How Beautiful. 27

Stormy Seas. 29

Promise 30

I Love you 33

Universe 34

New discovery 35

Hope. 36

Your Laugh 37

MY SOUL

Who are you? 41

Mirror 43

Robot 44

Pieces 46

Soar. 48

As mind of an artist 49

Reflection. 50

I am a girl. 52

River Flows 54

Unique 58

Story 59

MY LIFE

Silence 63

The Legend of the castle 64

Wishes 67

A shot 69

Lights out 70

Rain 72

Singing Stars 75

Caged. 77

MY MIND

Missing 81

Another Mirror 82

Goodbye 83

Try 84

Confetti 85

Never have I ever 87

Masked 88

Broken 90

Forgotten 91

Lonely 93

This feeling 95

Faded scars 97

Teardrops on my pages 98

Movie 100

Artist 102

Replaced 104

Grow Up 106

MY SENSE

Sight 109

I don't fit in 111

I want 113

Reality Hit 114

Window 116

Chipped 117

Grandfather Clock 119

Do people? 121

Women are weak 122

Dreams 125

MY HEART

The piece that bleeds every time it's with you

Masterpiece

Chipped, chipped, chipped
A chopped piece of my back
Chipped, chipped, chipped,
On he goes forming another crack

His chisel made my eyes
With features that made the world awe
But all I saw was the sadness in his
His story, his dreams and his flaws.

When he sculpted my ears
I could finally hear him speak
Sweet nothings, his cries, his promise
And how the moving world is a trick

When he made my nose
I finally smelled the everything
Stone, metals, wood and pain
Even his perfume in my surrounding

He made my legs and my arms
And put me in a beautiful dress
I now stood on my toes, my hands in the air
With my emotionless face and my hair in a mess

Finally he crafted my lips
And landed a feathered kiss
"Now, you dancer" his final words
"Have become my master piece"

I never saw him again
But I did see those eyes.
For I was a timeless masterpiece
In a world where time flies

Soulmate

I believed in soulmates before I met you
I no longer believe in them
I no longer believe in the fate
That one person in meant to be with me

That one person out there
Somewhere is my other half
Because if I did, that person
And that person wouldn't even measure up to you

So now I believe that soulmates don't exists
But are created
Little by little
Bit by bit
With every laugh and every struggle

We both mold into the perfect
Person for each other
We may not be soul mates
But we are perfect souls for each other

Hopeful

Maybe one day
Will be tomorrow
When we meet
And melt all our sorrows

When we hold
Our trembling hands
And leave our footprints
In the sand

Maybe we make promises
That we will never be able to keep
Only for the warmth
Both of us desperately seek

Bend the will of space and time
To gain time we do desire
Before the universe knows
That our love had set fires

Spend a few more moments with time
That was never ours but borrowed
Maybe one day we will
But why can't it be tomorrow

With You

The wind in my hair,
Longing rides,
Holding hands,
And starry nights

Our first rain,
With a cozy fireplace,
A book to read,
And your beautiful face

Bus rides,
Beside you,
Blurry rides,
Even at night too.

I love these scenes,
Till my heart's content,
But it's you that
My heart truly contains.

Each moment with you,
Is like a dream come true,
A world of beauty
A love so true.

I'll cherish these moments,
Forever in my heart,
And together we'll create
Our own work of art.

Mother

You were there to hear
my first word, laugh and cry
You were the one to teach me
the right from wrong, the truth from lie

You struggled a million times
but never complain once
My mother, my best friend
you shine brighter than a thousand suns

you laugh and cry with me
over voices rise higher when we fight
but my home will always feel empty
without you being my first sight

My criticized, inspiration and motivation
that is what you are
the reason for my success
even with you being far

Thank you ma
for being my hope
without you
life would be hard to cope

One final verse
but this is not the end
at the last hour of the end
I have you, a mother and a friend

I love you mum
and distance will never keep us apart
don't worry mum
I have you in my heart

❋ ❋ ❋

She said, "I wish that would happen,"
Longing for it to come her way.
He replied, "Me too,"
Desiring it to happen with her someday.
They wondered who loved more,
But the answer was crystal clear:
Their love for each other was equal,
And they held each other dear.

Friendship

Amazing thing
Friendship is
Some may end up cursed
But others bring us bliss

The feeling of belonging
Is the one that we want
The fear of losing a friend
Is one of thousand haunts

Secrets, laughs and love
May make friendship grow
But the real test is when
Your life tortures you soul until it's very low

See the song of friendship
Is amazing but hard to read
For one flick, one mistake
May ripped it with the seed

I've had many friends
In this lifetime
Some I have lost
Some I still call mine

The hardest thing to make is a friend
That's why we start very young
But even then we spend our life
Understanding the song that's already been already
sung

Maybe one day we'll find
True friends that love us
Friends that light the embers of our happiness
And turn sadness to dust

But for now I sing, Amazing thing
Friendship is
Some may end up cursed
But others bring us bliss

Love

You don't make my heart skip a beat
But you always put a smile on my face

I thought v were different
I thought I'd explore a new world with you
But when u reminded me "I haven't seen tomorrow
And neither have you"
I found out the truth about you

Honey
I though we different
But now I understand
We are holding on to the same string
Just at different ends

Darling,
My words mean nothing
If my actions cant prove
But I promise I'll try my best
To make this world better for you

Because i know how it feels
When you drown deep without a light
And cry yourself to sleep
In our darkest night

I believe in what you are
And seen what you can be
And I will help you swim
Through this dark sea

You and me

I can make walking on
Lego look painless
I can make life look like a beautiful chaos
Even if it's just a full me

I can wear a mask
And say "I'm fine"
When I see u with someone else
Even if u promised to be mine

I love you
But u never saw that
I trusted u
But u never trusted back

And now I'm here alone
Hoping for someone new
Even when I died
The day I left you

Sail

He wrote to me today
An ode to his righteous words
That felt like they had escape the worlds terror
Only to scarred several stories to unheard

His letter said
"Pain brought the stories of loss and the lonely
But love brought you forth
If pain were the foggy sea
You were my true north"

He wrote of his great adventures
And the lessons he had learnt
And ended with a reminder
That everyone has been burnt

With each word, he painted a picture,
Of adventures far and wide,
And though I had never seen it,
I could feel the world through his eyes.

I read on, captivated by his tale,
And as I reached the end,
I realized with a star.
That his love, too, he send

For thought he never spoke the words,
I could feel theme in every line.,
And suddenly, i knew it to be true,
That this love of his was mine.

And as I read that last letter,
Before the storm did pass,
I knew that i found my way,
To a love that would forever last

How Beautiful

Oh how beautiful may it be
To hold you hand
And walk side by side
To laugh and cry together
Even in the strongest tide

Never thinking of
What might happen to us
In the future
But only thinking about
How happy we are now

My life became dedicated
To the memories
We created together
Every song I listen to
Is a recollection
Of a moments we had

Oh how beautiful was life
At that time
At that moment,
In that second

I fell in love with you
And so did your soul
Fall in love with me
But sadly not all good things last
And neither did we

Stormy Seas

Look beside you, my love,
Cause that's where I'll be
When your life is bloom
Or going through the stormy seas

If you're scared
Hold my hand
And safe there you'll be
In my arms
I'll protect you
From the rough and stormy seas

Promise

Promises were just words
Until I made them with you
Future was always uncertain
Until we made plans with just
Me and you

I didn't think we would end like this
But maybe I was wrong
Maybe you trusted a wrong person
Who couldn't give you what you want

I'm sorry for every pain I have caused
And I know I don't deserve to be forgiven
But maybe just once more
We could use the connection
To come together like we were driven

If your answer is yes
I'll be whatever you want in a girl
If you answer is no
Well then don't worry you won't see my crashing
world

I promised to love you
And I intend to keep that promise
Even if we just become a story that starts with
Once upon a time there was us

❋ ❋ ❋

"How do you know when you're in love?"

"You never truly know when you're in love,"

"Love is the happiness you feel when you look at yourself and the world seems brighter.

It's the voice inside you that urges you to be your best.

It's the fluttering feeling in your heart when you think of that one person, and the ache when they're not there.

Love is not just a passing feeling, but a force that runs deep in your veins, it's something you feel in your bones and your soul.

They say love grows stronger with every challenge it withstands, And you'll only know it when you feel it in your heart, not just in your mind."

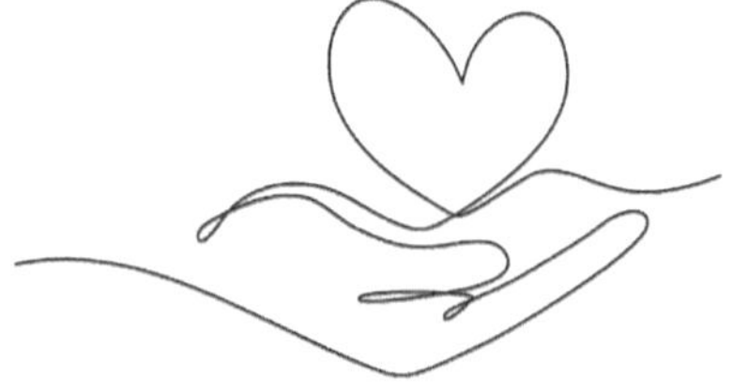

I Love you

You know
I love you
But I'm scared to
Admit it to myself too

My love for you is true
And something out of this world
So beautiful yet chaotic
That can't be described in words

Your love is so rare
I want you to stay
But I screw it every time
Rather than say I what I need to say

You are perfect all round
And I'm broken everywhere
Those combinations are amazing
But also pack a scare

But I know you'll love me
No matter what
I hope this valentine you remember
'Cause I love you a lot

Universe

If I love you in one universe
I love you in all of them
You understand me in a way
The rest of them couldn't then

I watched as your walked in the room
And lit it up like a star being born
But your eyes only lit up when
they saw someone they couldn't scorn

Take my hand and Vll dance
Slowly to the sweet melody
My love hold me close
In your arms ever so sweetly

Close our eyes and watch the darkness
Succumb us in a different lie
Your arms brought me back to light
To a world with you and I

I wished to grow with you At New Years
And wished we have a tomorrow with every
shooting star
Wish we stay here together
To ever the galaxies away and far

New discovery

Spent hours thinking
How I feel abt u
Wasted hours watching
No words breaking through

Consumed by the feeling
U spread through me
These feelings I keep inside
Never setting them free

No amount of words
Can describe this feeling
Nervous, excited, scared
Or maybe even thrilling

Like discovering a new color
And loving it just the same
I was a willing pawn
Playing your game

Hope

We were young and naive when we began here,
Protected by four walls from the harsher sphere,
Unaware of the struggles that awaited us outside,
But gazing out the window, we saw a world in its
pride.

We admired the beauty and the grandeur of it all,
But when it turned cold, we retreated to our walls,
Innocent and unprepared, we chose to hide,
Hoping to one day be ready to venture outside.

We now realize that we were too young to
comprehend,
The difficulties and hardships that life could send,
But we made a pact to face the real world together,
And conquer every obstacle, come whatever.

Your Laugh

I no longer count rose petals,
Nor read romantic books with their mottos.
I've stopped criticizing myself in the mirror,
Hoping that you'd take notice and draw nearer.

I have loved you, still do, and always will,
But it seems that you'll never know how I feel.
I hope that someday you'll find a love like mine,
And that it won't go unnoticed or be left behind.

It's ironic, I suppose, to long for things out of reach,
To love someone who won't love you back, so to
speak.
Yet, I knew that I loved you from the start,
The day I made you laugh and touched your heart.

MY SOUL

The piece that shines when I am my truest self

Who are you?

I begin with
I'm my fathers daughter
I'm my mothers friend
I'm my brothers sister
And boyfriends girlfriend

I am a sister
for all my friends
And a conduit for their anger
For those who pretend

For some I am their home
For others I am a rock
The list goes on
And never ends at a stop

I am the struggles I have faced
I am the past they can't erased

I am a mixture of people That I meet everyday
And when you combine all those things
You finally see me in every way

So who am I?
I am a part of you
I am everything I want be
Every struggle and happiness made this
I am me

Mirror

Hey there mirror
I have to ask you
I know life will be hard
But will I make it through?

I look at u with a smile upon my face
And I look at you after I cry
You ve seen me at my lowest point
And you have seen me wanting to touch the sky

So mirror why won't you answer me
If I am strong enough to make it through
You reflect my pain and happiness
So I believe in your judgment too

I'll be honest with you mirror
I'm scared of the person I'll be
Scared that I'll one day wake up
And won't recognise who I see

So I'll go now, still, afraid
But with you by my side
I remember the lesson you taught me
'I'm stronger when I have nothing to hide'

Robot

I'm not a robot
Following everything you say
I'm not a robot
Following your footprints day by day

What did I do
That was so wrong?
All I did was follow my heart
And sing my own song

Robots can't think
Or have their own voice
Because you command them
And take away their choice

You told me that
I could never be more
That if I try to fly
I would sink instead of soar

But all that did
Was made me dream bigger
Flying higher than I was
Before when I was bounded by fear

I'm not a robot
And I never will be
I love being a human
And having a capacity of thinking freely

Pieces

A collection of pieces
Of the broken fragments of my soul
Each piece holds a story
A dream, a wish, a memory and so much more

Maybe many have tried
To put them together like they were before
But let me tell you the pieces won't fit
Because I am not who I was anymore

Believe me when I say
I am happy as I am
I am broken but stronger and smarter now
A wolf rather than a lamb

Before one word wrong
Would spiral in me to cry
Now a hundred knives in my back
I smile and watch others try

Like a broken clock
Something people have never seen
My story is hidden but the collections
Are glimpses of how I have been

I, a broken girl, in a beautiful world
Trying to keep my struggles behind my eyes
Am glad to see I am not alone
I am just one of many that tries

Soar

I give u everything you want
I do everything for you
If tomorrow you ask me to give you my soul
I'll give it to you too

But u should know
Everyday is a struggle for me
Everyday all I try is to make it to the next

Life should be about living
But I'm not living anymore
All i'm trying to do is survive
Until the day I'm strong enough to soar

As mind of an artist

A restless mind of an artist
Is never one to sit still
A restless mind of an artist
Always finding holes to fill

A restless mind of an artist
Finding cracks that are never there
A restless mind of an artist
Making sure their hands are never bare

A restless mind of an artist
Comes from with in their soul
They accept this restlessness
And make creativity their goal

Reflection

She looks in the mirror
And cusses at her own reflection
Wondering when
Will she finally get that satisfaction?
He looks at her
And all he sees is beauty
Wondering why she treats herself
With such cruelty.

Her best friend looks at her and loves her
For who she is and has always been
She looks at her as she does her own sister
A person for someone to hold and on whom to lean

Her parents look at her
With such admiration
Never hoping for anything
As she exceeded all their expectations.

The girls she called friends
Were nothing but jealous of her
For when her beauty and smarts were compared
To them, they were seen as failures

Many knew her
As the girl who has everything
Yet when she saw herself in the mirror
She struggled to see anything.

The lesson we must all learn
Is to never see a person as subjective
Cause everything in the world is based
On someone else's perspective

I am a girl

I am a girl
I am a daughter
I am a sister
I am a friend
I am a wife
But that's not it

Like the earth
I have many layers
Sweet and kind from the outside
But inside I am a Dragon slayer

Being a girl
Isn't a curse or a burden
It's a blessing
And that I am certain

I may not know many things
But I have been taught several

Being a sister
Gave me an opportunity
For being responsible for another
Being a daughter
Made me have respect
For everyone like no other

Being a friend
Taught me to share
Being a wife
Taught me to care

So if you find yourself
Asking 'why are you a girl'?
Just remember
A girl has the whole world

River Flows

"What makes you think you can be a writer"

Those stony words
Pierced through my skin.
I didn't know that after all this time
It was still like ice, fragile and thin.

And then it all came back
Rushing through my veins into me
Like branches of river
All flowing into the sea

Now everyday I wake up
To the question they asked me
And what I do next unconsciously, is simple
I scribble my thoughts into poetry

I hover over the paper with the pen I hold,
But nothing flows out
The hesitance of the words
Sink me in even deeper doubt.

What makes me think I can be a writer?
I sigh and dim down the lights.

They say that I have no stories to tell
Or a talent I wish I could sell.

They say "to be a writer
Is to feel emotions deep within"
They tell me my personality
It is like ice on water on a chilly day, so shallow and
thin.

But they don't know
What it takes to smile all the time
When there are thousands things that can break you
and thousand people who won't give a dime.

What they don't know is that I do have a story
Like everyone in this land
A story some will never know
A story only few will understand

My story is about a girl
Who tries to smiles everyday
A story of a girl who hopes that her smile
Could light someone else's way

It's about a girl,
Who is in her own way a fighter
With a pen as her gun and words as bullets
She becomes a writer. :,) so beautiful

It's about a girl
Who turns her bleeding pain
Into words that
Flow like a river in rain

And that's whats makes me a writer
If you don't already know
My words, like my emotions, pour out
Like the river flows

❊ ❊ ❊

I've journeyed through a thousand deaths,

To leave behind my former self.

Lived a thousand lives before,

To find my truth, my inner wealth.

Loved a thousand times before,

To realize I am enough, nothing else.

This life, this moment, is where I stand,

To embrace the journey and take command.

Unique

I'm not original
But I'm unique
I keep collecting pieces of others
And add them to me as we speak

Like a blank canvas
I start with white
Then I add a little of
Darkness of the night

Then I add the color of
Every person I care
Even if they leave, I'll have
A part of them, always, there

At first glance
I might seem like a mess
But I'm just a puzzle of art
With several different pieces

Story

Every character in a book
Has a story to tell. I don't.
I have hundreds, thousands
As many as you can comprehend

My stories are not only my own
They come from every relationship I have sown
From every struggle I have faced
To every pain I have known

I will not restrict myself to a story
That make me look like a hero
When in reality I have been
A villain, a loser, a zero
In someone else's

Why would I restrict myself
To one story when I lived and loved so many
Each as special as the others
Is now part of my identity

MY LIFE

The piece that could never compare to other

❋ ❋ ❋

When the sky falls down
And the stars explode
When you see the deepest cracks
Where the river flowed

You will remember only
Of what you love and lost
Your bonds will shatter
Like thin ice in frost

When you kneel down
Begging this world to take you
You will see the dust and ashes
Where stood the world you once knew

It may not be today
And it may not be tomorrow
But the day will come
Where you will have to feel
the sorrow

Silence

I have a lot to say
But silence is gold
Learning from mistakes
And not the lessons told

But some words hold power
Pure and strong like diamonds
With the right amount of pressure
To have a will to defeat thousand

So don't mistake my isolation,
It's solely because I'm waiting
For my words to be ready
Before they start debating

For I fear if I speak too soon
My pain will be futile
Diamonds take long to be made
So I offer you my silence a while

The Legend of the castle

This is a lesson, a legend, a story
Of a once glorious castle now broken
Of a time when everyone knew
Swords were weaker than words spoken

The strength of the castle, unmatched
Until the changing of the tides
Swords couldn't do the damage
That the mere words did from outside

They catapulted like boulders and bombs
Onto the castles beautiful stone walls
The words had power to break the castle
And watch it wailing, as it crumbles and falls

The castle now lay in dust and ash
A reminder of what it used to be
But don't you fret or mourn the castle
As it is not the end of this story

The legend whispers of the people who stood strong
Who chose to fight and not run
Against all odds, they held their ground
With every step, they stood their own

May the sky fall down or the stars explode
The people of the castle wouldn't hide
they knew that the castle was just walls
To keep the real strength of the army inside

So let the winds howl and the storm rage
The castle may fall but not its brave,
For they will stand tall, proud and bold,
Forever remember, their story told

❋ ❋ ❋

Have you ever rode a bike at night
When there is no one on the road
Except the trucks
Carrying their cargo

Wen the only shops open
Are the medicals on the streets
When the rain has gone yet
You feel drops gravitating down ur cheeks

Wen the only sound you hear
Are the owls hooting and the whispers of the wind
Have you ever see a tree light up
With all the fireflies twinkling within

Have you seen the city fall asleep
From a view only a few will ever know
Have you ever rode a bike at night
When there is no one on the road

Wishes

I wished up a shooting star
And I heard him laugh
"Do you still believe in those things?"
Smirkingly he asked.

"Why won't I?" I asked him

"I believe in the shooting stars
That fall from the sky
I make a wish at 11:11
At night when the world passes me by

I make a wish on the candles
Of my birthday cake
And wish on the wishbones
Right before it breaks

I believe our destinies are written
But we can still change our fates
And yes if you are wondering
I do believe in soulmates.

I have hope and faith
In everything that I do
So why don't you tell me
What is that you believe into"

He stood there with his mouth agape
And his eyes open wide
And then he spoke words
That reignited my flutters inside

"I believed in you
From the day we met from the bottom of my heart
Because you were able to believe
That the darkness of the world could be set apart

My belief in you
Grew strong everyday
So I apologize
If my beliefs are different from yours
But I still love you in every way"

A shot

A shot of sunset
For all the time together we would spend
A reminder that life isn't a fairytale
And all good things come to an end

A shot of moon
In hopes it's watching over you
So when I look at it
I see you staring at it too

A shot of twilight
With all its stars shining for centuries
Remember the nights we spent under then
Sharing our stories?

A shot of sunrise
A reminder of our fates twine
A lesson hard to forget
That you were never meant to be mine

Lights out

The cloak of darkness
That came over
Vanished every bit of light
As we managed to take cover

We embraced the silence
As they took control
Our voice and words
Were turned to dust n coal

We sat there listening to
our heavy breathing
Battling the silence
And we closed our eyes
to get the world to make sense

We felt our fears take over
We didn't know who was whispering in the dark
We were too scared to open our eyes
Until we saw a spark

We didn't know
What happened when
The darkness came out
But our hope was returned
When the light came erasing doubt

✳ ✳ ✳

Life's twists and turns make it more thrilling,

Bumps around each corner, like a rollercoaster spinning.

In the midst of lightning and thunder's sound,

Snuggling with our loved ones, comfort we found.

We watched the rain, as it pooled around us,

Dragging us towards the trenches, a treacherous fuss.

But we knew that as long as we had something to live for,

We'd never stay too long in the depths and lore.

Rain

I hope you trickle down
From every leave of every tree
Finally onto the ground
That absorbs thee

You bring life as a gift
In your small god given bodies
Vibrantly brighten up every dull green
What's more that this honorable deeds

You rise the levels of the lakes and seas
Give the humans places inside you
You carry the weight of the world Yet you float
Sometime it feels as though you are too good to be
true

It's sometimes unclear why humans wish upon
falling stars
When you a part of their earth
You have seen everything on this land
Since god gave you birth

You have seen their history
and seen their mistakes
You have imprinted on them, making roads
As you trickle down their faces

They have danced with you
And fell in love as you fell down
They have forgotten how you have comforted them
Just by your falling sound

You are a drop in a million
And a million drops in you
There may be a few that hate
But also a few that fell in love with you

Close your eyes and let the flashlights pass,
Drown out the sorrow and the noise of the past.
Open your eyes to the night sky above,
Reflecting the beauty in each sparkle and love.

Gaze up and see the stars shining bright,
Their beams giving you a reason to delight.
What once brought you sorrow and despair,
Is now your hope and promise for a better tomorrow
to share.

Close your eyes again, and let the world go,
Feel the peacefulness and let your spirit flow.
Breathe in and out, and let yourself be free,
Embracing the beauty and the tranquility.

Singing Stars

Do you think
The stars see the song
That is in your heart
Or the symphony
That is released when your
Soul is ripped apart.

Everyday,
She waited for someone to listen
To listen to her soul music
But like a forgotten melody
She was left in a corner, unheard.

After all these years
When her soul played the chord
The stars heard her notes
And ask her to sing
At the final note of her song
Her heart was finally shining

She waited for someone to pick her up
But when no one showed up
She let her soul be bottled up

But Today something happened,
She didn't wait for someone else's cheer
Because today she heard
The stars, singing "for you I am always here"

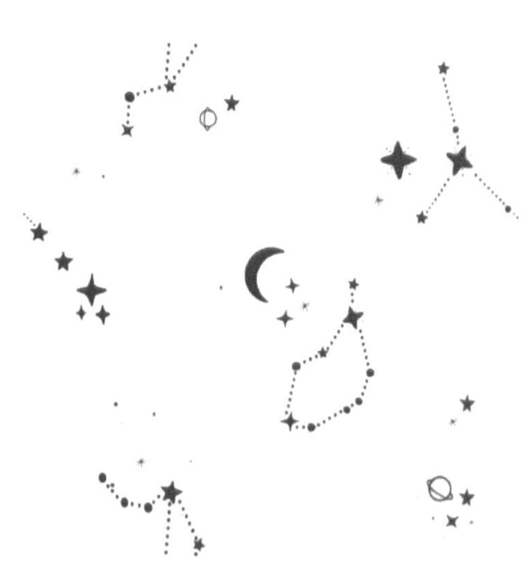

Caged

Imagine a bird
Who couldn't fly,
Crashed on the ground
Away from the sky.

In front of her are bars
That circled around her making a cage,
She chirps for help
Until her sadness turns into rage.

She flaps her wings against the cage
Hoping for someone to hear,
Because the mere thought of her freedom in flames
Makes her break down in tears.

Soon she gives up
Never hoping again to be set free,
Now imagine that bird
Is to be someone like you and me

MY MIND

A quiet piece of mine that explodes time to time

Missing

All it took was one song.
One song to remind me that
My life will never be the same

I just laid there as
Memories passed through my head
People, places, adventures
All of them

As years started passing in front of my eyes
One by one the memories started to fade
As though with every tear
that escapes my eyes
My memories start to fall
Shatter like glass into a million pieces
Too small to put them back together

I miss
Getting lost into unknown cities wid u
Looking at the city light like v do
See the sky change from red to blue
I miss you... Do you miss me too?

Another Mirror

I look at it
As it looks at me
It's a reflection on a mirror
What else could it be

I yell at it
And it yells at me.
It's a reflection on a mirror
What else could it be

I look away
And its looks away like me
It's a reflection on a mirror
What else could it be

I stare at the crack
That now makes broken mirror whole
Still the cracks are seen
Like darkness luring in a hole

The mirror temps me
To speak my deepest fear
And it looks back
As I break down in tears

Goodbye

You say you love me
But you don't show it
From the day we met
Till our last meet

You say you know me
But how can that be true
Cause you were the first one to runaway
When my life turned blue

You promised to stay forever
But somehow that changed
Now when I look at you
I see someone strange

It's mysterious how people
so close Can drift so far
With one word
We were miles apart

And don't try to come back
When my life is good
I am stronger and smarter now
But no thanks to you

Try

The more I let out
The more it hurts

The more I get out my anger
The more pain I feel

The more I try to feel myself
The more I feel out of place

The more I try to get out of my head
The more it all comes crashing down on me

I try try and try again
But I always fail
I'm sorry but I'm giving up
'Cause I'd rather not try than get hurt

Got more emotion
Than I know what to Do with
Maybe once I'll feel again
But for now I'm done trying

Confetti

If I could only explode
You would finally see me
Spilling around you
Like a million little confetti

Anger red would shout at you
To show you the anger I keep inside
In The blue confetti you would see
How many tears I have cried

The green ones would show you
The wars I lost after my fight
The black paper would show you
How many times I hv lost my sight

The yellow ones are for all
My hopes and dreams
The grays ones are storage
For my nightmare and screams

In the end you would find
some white confetti in your hair
That's what I am at my core
The purest part of me but no one seems to care

If I could only explode
You would finally see me
Spilling around you
Like a million little confetti

Never have I ever

Never have I ever
Felt left out
Never ever I ever
Had a feeling out doubt

Never have I ever
let someone break my trust
Never have I ever
Felt myself disgust

Never have I ever
Hated myself
Never have I ever
Hated someone else

Never have I ever
lied
Never have I ever
Until this time

Masked

I wipe my tears
But my nose is still red
I hope nobody notices it
But I hope somebody does

I say "I'm fine"
But my voice comes out shaky
I hope nobody notices it
But I hope someone does

I hide my hands behind my back
Which are trembling anxiously
I hope nobody notices it
But I hope somebody does

It's not because I'm looking for attention
That I don't say anything
But I have learned lying
To answer "how have you been?"

I have heard a great many times
That no one really wants to know
How you are or if you are alright
So don't let your emotions show

But I don't hide anything
From the world, you see
You could see the cracks of my soul
If you really cared about me

Lying, as I learned
Is a better answer to the question, masked
But the truth and silence
Are the answers to the questions you never asked

Broken

One look at me
You see I'm broken
You keep me in a corner
And leave me unspoken

Days, months, years pass by
But no one came to look
Forgotten little me
Like an old book

Am I so broken,
That I can't be fixed?
Am I so lost
That I can't be found?

Why you leave me
Is not my question to ask
I'll just continue being broken
Carrying on wearing a mask

Forgotten

The world forgets me, a mere ghost
Lost in the sea of life's vast coast
I stand before them. But unseen
A shadow in the background. Routine

I once thought they'd hear my voice
That they'd see me. And make a choice
To understand and empathize
But to them. I'm A mere disguise

I blend in like a whisper in the wind
A face in the crowd. Easy to rescind
I smile and wave. My emotion masked
My loneliness ignored, my pain surpassed

I am a lighthouse lost in the storm
A ship that's tossed. broken and worn
Invisible to those who pass by
A forgotten soul. Who's left to die

While I'm but a drop in the sea
I still yearn to be seen and free
To find a place where I belong
Where I'm not just a forgotten song

✳ ✳ ✳

My mind creates endless scenarios,
Leaving me unsure which path to take.
Life becomes a tangled web of confusion,
As I struggle to determine the right choice to make.

I am aware that loving you
Will only bring me pain and strife.
It's a battle I've fought countless times,
With no hope of treasure to find in this life.

Despite the lessons I've learned along the way,
When it comes to you, my heart and head collide.
I couldn't care less about the consequences,
My emotions and thoughts are forever entwined.

Lonely

She had many names she was called by
But never the name she wanted to hear
She wanted to live the life of truth but couldn't
Though she could see all the loneliness crystal clear

She wanted to reach out; grab someone
And show them the truth
That life not lived the way it was meant to be
Was like a tree without a blossom or a fruit

So one day she jumped up on stage
And spoke to every person that was lonely
That life maybe a tiring game
But it's not a game to play solely

She said
"It's been a thing everyone's known for a while
But never said anything, that it's strange
That the only constant in life
The constant change

We sit, we stand, we walk, we breathe
Our day consists of the change
So why can't our life be

Why should we suffer the dark of the lonely?
Why should we suffer lonely and depressed?
Why can't our voice be ours to speak
We should our souls be suppressed"

She got off stage and saw the first lonely person
And spoke words that lifted the situation before it
worsened
"You are lonely but so am I
Everyone's lonely so why can't we try
Try to do well for us and others
Being human is a boon not a curse

Life is unpredictable but with the right people by
your side
Maybe we can survive life's Never ending tide"

This feeling

Do u ever feel
Like you body will just shut down
The load of the world so heavy
That you sink into the ground

You felt when their words
Catapult on your castle walls
Waiting for a moment of weakness
So your glorious castle falls

It feels like being suffocated
Under the deepest trenched water
Wanting to survive
But no means to fight harder

It's like sinking in quicksand
And getting dragged beneath
And you know once you let go
There's no escaping the darkness within

I don't know how to fight this feeling
Don't know if I ever would
I'll drown, suffocate, even crumble
Until I fall where I stood

I'm so tired of fighting
A war that can't be won
I'm just hoping that I'll make it
to watch another dawn

Faded scars

I carve the roads on my skin.
Scribble words with my blood ink.

I feel the land crippling down.
I fall in darkness but make no sound.

Could it be the answers to questions asking,
answers who lie deep in the hole; wondering.

Lonely and scared then cold and numb,
Sooner or later the darkness succumbs ".

The only way out, follow the star,
High in the sky, out of reach, too far.

I'll stay here instead of reaching,
With the fear of failure that keeps crawling.

But one day I'll reach the star,
That day I won't look at my faded scars.

Teardrops on my pages

As I write this
I shed the last of my tears
Believing in a brighter future
And many happy years

These last few years taught me
Lessons very hard
Repeated my mistakes over and over again
Until I learnt them by heart

These last few tears
Are for the ones who left
A robbery of my broken pieces
But never a reported theft

These tears that are now
A part of the pages I write
Are proof that I didn't give in
When it was a tough fight

So let's leave it there
The knowers know
Who they are
But will never show

A thanks to them
For leaving me in cages
Because of them
I have teardrops on my pages

Movie

She was the main character
In her own movie life
She would dance under stars, in the rain
As the world would pass her by

And like in every movie
She found her love interest
A tall beautiful man
Whose emotions reflected herselves

They fell for each other
Under the same sky she dance
While the stars sung their songs
And they both go captivated in a trance

You could see their love
Shining from miles away
But they weren't just shining, but burning
And then came one faithful day

He broke their promises
Without telling her he left
He broke down her walls
He was a thief, her soul he had theft

She loved him for a long time
And hope he would come back
Bring her soul to her
Bring the light her world lacked

Soon she learned a difficult lesson
That changed her deeply
Now she danced under the stars
Hiding from her own movie

She was a main character
In her life which she loved as a movie
Only now she had learned that life
Isn't that kind of fantasy story

Artist

I am an artist
You see
I criticize my own work
To make sure it's good as it can be

When we started
I promised myself
Your love won't be the death of me

But your words
Your sweet innocent words
Made me fall and fall n fall for your love

Then your late replies
Suffocated me
Like I was drowning in
Beneath the sea

Our busy life
Rushed past us
You know the terrifying feeling you get
When you stand too close to a moving train or a bus?

Soon enough I knew
Your love would never be the death of me

It was you you and only you
That could kill me

But I hope you don't
And like a hopeless romantic
I fall even more for you
And I know you won't

Replaced

I don't feel like I exist
Like I matter in anybody's life

Till this day I wonders
If anybody thinks about me
If anybody wonder where I'll be

I make them laugh
I make them smile
Sometimes I'm the shoulder
They cry on for a while

But that doesn't matter
'Cause I'm replaceable...

They throw me
When they want

They leave me in a corner of their house
And forget about me
When I look in their eyes
It's not love I see

It's the feeling of annoyance I get
"when will she leave"?

'Cause they think they'll be happier without me

But for me,
I love them all
N maybe one day
That will be my down fall

'Cause they don't know
That I cannot replace them
'Cause the memories I cherish will always be the
same

Grow Up

Yes, I am selfish,
But what are you going to do about it?
I am getting what I want
While you act like a child throwing a fit

Life was hard enough
With fake people to sort through
But leaving me was the best thing you did
So… well done and thank you!

You can whisper behind my back
And spread rumors about me
But I am a shining star!
You can't outshine me baby!

I finally understand why hell was empty
The devils, they ran from you
They survived but now you are here
Don't you ever get a clue?

See, you think you can win this
But why not think outside your range?
You are a bratty child in an adult world
Why don't you try growing up for a change?

MY SENSE

A piece of how I see the world

Sight

She lost her sight at an age,
where she had just started seeing the truth.
She took the loss of her sight hard,
Harder in her youth.

She thought seeing the world
Would make her a part of it
That not seeing would keep her apart
and tear her spirit.

Her brain had stopped
Her heart was broken
Her sight was lost
She thought her fate was woven

So she sat there in a chain
For days and months at most
Away from everyone,
With doors and windows closed

You see what she didn't learn was that she could see
More things than this world had known
And her surroundings had bent to her desires
To make her feel at home.

She didn't know that she could she
More colors than one could ever seek.
So many more colors
That could leave this world bleak.

Soon she learned that
The truth about the world isn't whether or not she
can see
It Is to adapt to what is given
And to nurture it to what it can be.

I don't fit in

It's funny when u say
That u care,
But your actions
They tell a different story.

U show me I don't fit in.
I don't fit in
With you and your group.
I never have and never will.

I feel like I HV been placed
In the middle of a game;
I don't really know what's happening.

I try my best to laugh with you,
But at the end of the day
I know I don't fit in.

U say I made a difference
But who are we kidding,
We all know the difference I made
Was only a distraction for you.

I know I don't fit in
But it still hurts.
Cause I still fight for you,
When I know you won't fight for me too.

I want

I want to change the world,
But they tell me I don't have that much power.
I want to make a difference,
But they say I'm too young.
I want to leave my mark,
But they say I can't.
They say I'm too weak
They say I'm not capable to do it

They say and say and say
But does that really matter?
Do their voices make me any less,
Than what I am?
What I want to be?
What I can be?

Do their voices and their trophies decide,
How my life should be shaped?
What is the point of my life?
What am I really here for?

Reality Hit

Life is not kind to all
And we all know how that's like
It sets us on a roller coaster
To make us tremble in fright

Those who play life as a game
Think they can win or lose
But there's more to stake than humiliation
A price you'd never choose

Those who dare to look past life
Are called insane, mental cases
But they see that life is more than them
Not heroes, but characters with no faces

But everyone has a role to play
At least that's what we like to believe
So we act the heroes
And find answers that we seek

But life is an entity
So divine and powerful that for most
Chasing it isn't possible
You'd be chasing a ghost.

So Shoutout to the victims of life
I finally know how it feels
To be a whole but still broken
To have scars that don't heal

Window

Look through your window
What have you seen?
Sky above, ground below
And people in between

I have seen them stare at each other
While many whisper and tall talk
Some don't even notice
How others behave and walk

Everyone has a story
Etched like a band
Roads of story drawn
In the palm of their hands

I have a small window
But it's the world I have seen
That it may be chaos put there
But it's where life is happening

Chipped

Another day.
Another piece of me,
Chipped away.

Sculpted by life
Chipped. But a masterpiece.
Even then, my voice echos
"You are still a monster, a beast"

Another day.
Another piece of me,
Chipped away.

Like water
No color to my soul.
Yet shards spread everywhere.
The price at life's toll.

Another day.
Another piece of me,
Chipped away.

Always wanted to be the first
But while pressure turned everyone to diamonds
I'll be turned to dust.

Final day.
Final piece of me,
Chipped away.

Now I am perfection
But staring back at me
I don't recognize my own reflection

Grandfather Clock

The silence is lonely
Lonelier then the darkness

In darkness I couldn't see anyone
In the silence I know there are others
And yet lonely is what I feel

We look for perfection
While the inner us withers away
Innocence only looks good for a child
Isn't that what they say?

Piece by piece the inner us thrown away
Like lost pieces of puzzle out of the box
And we don't realize it until it's too late
When we hear the chimes of the grandfather clock

We grow up to be
A product of society around us
A perfectly independent individual
With no one left to trust

The innocence we felt
Flew away like birds in a flock
And we don't realize it until it's too late
When we hear the chimes of the grandfather clock

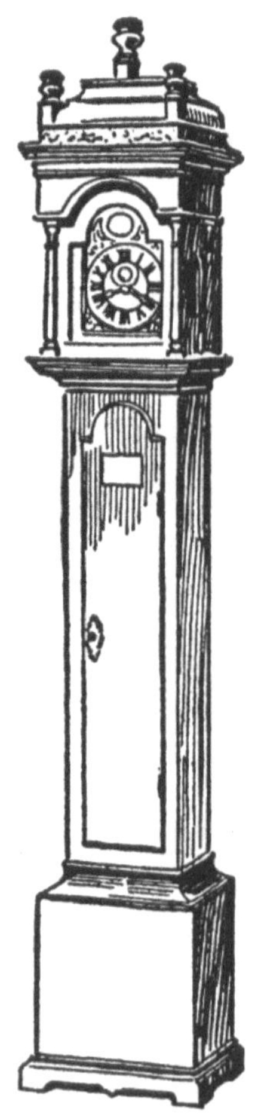

Do people?

Do people still care
For their happy ending?
Or just run behind whatever
That is now trending?

Do people care about being
Happy in life?
They why do you suppose
Hundreds cut their wrist with a knife?

Do people still strive
To find and fight for someone they love?
Or do they lock that part of themselves
Like all the other emotions they did before

Do people care about others?
Because i see so many people on the streets
But no one seemed bothered?

Humans have grown
Into something beautiful
But we gave up what we fought for
So now we are just fools

Women are weak

We women work hard
On how we look
We work hard
To be by the book

To make sure Our bodies the right size
Our skin the perfect hue
But darling don't get us wrong
'Cause none of it is for you

We do it for ourselves
Our confidences and our lives
Is it really hard to imagine
We want to be more than someone's wives?

We want to be rich
So we won't depend on anyone
We want to be famous
To inspire others with what we have done

We don't live for your needs
And we don't dress for your satisfaction
We love our bodies, our mind and our soul
And your opinion are a mere fraction

But the truth is even today
Women makes a cent to every dollar a man makes
This world makes us feel
That being a women is our biggest mistakes

No one lives forever
But that doesn't mean we shouldn't live at all
Our lives are not ours to live
From the day they made our call

We are not meant to dress freely
We are not meant stay out late
Our lives are just tethered to someone
Until we are old n then it's too late

We are meant to be the perfect gender
The one with bolds and beauty
But we leave our education
To fulfill our "rightful" duty

You call us weak
Because you have heard our cries
But those tears are the results of boiling anger
That pours out of our eyes

We are judged by everyone
For our looks and kindness
But we hope one day the world will open up
To care for our mindfulness

Our lives are not the faint of heart
And you won't find the answers in a book
Just remember this the next time you complain
To a women worrying about her looks

We may not have all the answers
But we hv the first the ones that you seek
So don't you ever dare say that
Women are weak

Dreams

The world's most powerful things,
Not knowledge, love, or money brings,
It's in the little things we call dreaming,
A power that's truly worth believing.

Our knowledge helps us light the way,
While love helps our dreams to stay,
Money can't buy what we aspire,
It's the dreams that truly inspire.

When we dare to dream,
Life's crossroads are what we'll glean,
We'll have a choice to make,
To see what's at stake.

Dreams may be hard to chase,
But they're worth it in the race,
A road without twists and turns,
Is like a bird that never learns.

Some people don't dare to dream,
Afraid of what others may deem,
But losing the beauty in their eyes,
It is like living life in a disguise.

When you find a dream that's true,
Hold on and see it through,
Follow it until the end of the world,
Even if everything else unfurled.

Don't be afraid to try,
Or to spread your wings and fly,
Dreams like yours are rare,
So dream of what you want and dare.

Dreams are what make life so sweet,
They make us feel so complete,
Dreams of trying, dreams of flying,
Dreams that are truly worth trying.

And now we become strangers again….